**Blastoff! Readers** are carefully developed by literacy experts to build reading stamina and move students toward fluency by combining standards-based content with developmentally appropriate text.

**Level 1** provides the most support through repetition of high-frequency words, light text, predictable sentence patterns, and strong visual support.

**Level 2** offers early readers a bit more challenge through varied sentences, increased text load, and text-supportive special features.

**Level 3** advances early-fluent readers toward fluency through increased text load, less reliance on photos, advancing concepts, longer sentences, and more complex special features.

★ **Blastoff! Universe**

This edition first published in 2024 by Bellwether Media, Inc.

No part of this publication may be reproduced in whole or in part without written permission of the publisher. For information regarding permission, write to Bellwether Media, Inc., Attention: Permissions Department, 6012 Blue Circle Drive, Minnetonka, MN 55343.

Library of Congress Cataloging-in-Publication Data

Names: Barnes, Rachael, author.
Title: Great gray owls / by Rachael Barnes.
Description: Minneapolis, MN : Bellwether Media, Inc., 2024. | Series: Blastoff! Readers. Who's hoo? Owls! | Includes bibliographical references and index. | Audience: Ages 5-8 | Audience: Grades 2-3 | Summary: "Relevant images match informative text in this introduction to great gray owls. Intended for students in kindergarten through third grade"-- Provided by publisher.
Identifiers: LCCN 2023008913 (print) | LCCN 2023008914 (ebook) | ISBN 9798886874150 (library binding) | ISBN 9798886876031 (ebook)
Subjects: LCSH: Great gray owl--Juvenile literature.
Classification: LCC QL696.S83 B37 2024  (print) | LCC QL696.S83  (ebook) | DDC 598.9/7--dc23/eng/20230320
LC record available at https://lccn.loc.gov/2023008913
LC ebook record available at https://lccn.loc.gov/2023008914

Text copyright © 2024 by Bellwether Media, Inc. BLASTOFF! READERS and associated logos are trademarks and/or registered trademarks of Bellwether Media, Inc.

Editor: Rebecca Sabelko     Designer: Brittany McIntosh

Printed in the United States of America, North Mankato, MN.

# Table of Contents

| | |
|---|---|
| Tall and Fluffy | 4 |
| Listening for Rodents | 12 |
| Beyond Hunting | 18 |
| Glossary | 22 |
| To Learn More | 23 |
| Index | 24 |

# Tall and Fluffy

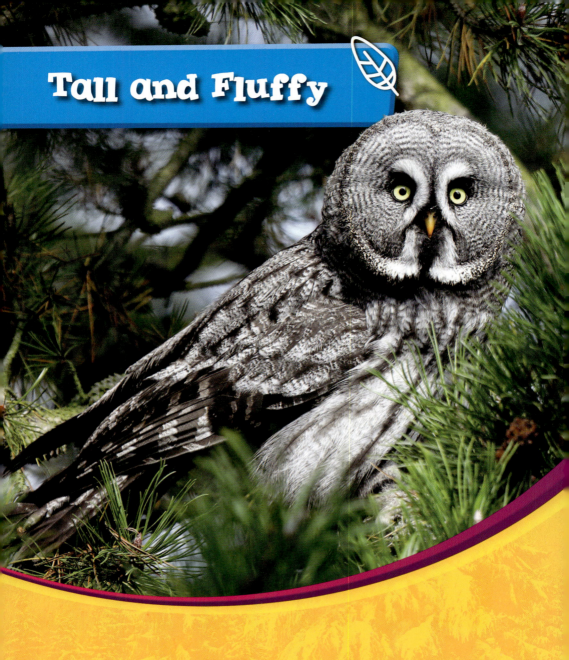

Great gray owls live in forests in northern parts of the world.

They have gray, white, and brown feathers. White feathers on their necks look like a bow tie!

### Great Gray Owl Range

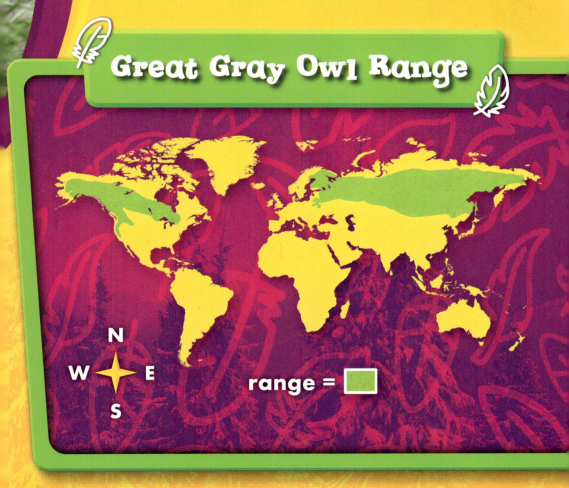

range =

Great gray owls have round faces.

Their eyes and beaks are yellow. Light feathers make an X between their eyes.

They are tall owls. They can reach 33 inches (84 centimeters) in height.

Their fluffy feathers make them look big. But they weigh less than 4 pounds (1.8 kilograms)!

## Spot a Great Gray Owl!

round face

yellow eyes and beak

fluffy feathers

long tail feathers

Great gray owls' **wingspans** can reach up to 5 feet (1.5 meters) wide!

When they fly, their long tail feathers look like a fan.

### Great Gray Owl Wingspan

0 — 1 foot — 3 feet — 5 feet

up to 5 feet (1.5 meters) wide

# Listening for Rodents

Great gray owls use their excellent hearing to hunt.

They can hear **rodents** move under deep snow!

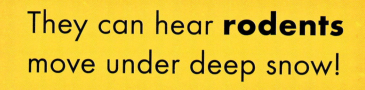
rodent

They often hunt from **perches**. They also hunt while flying silently over **meadows**.

When they hear **prey**, they dive! They grab rodents with their sharp **talons**.

perch

talons

## Great Gray Owl Food

lemmings

voles

**Raptors** attack young great gray owls.

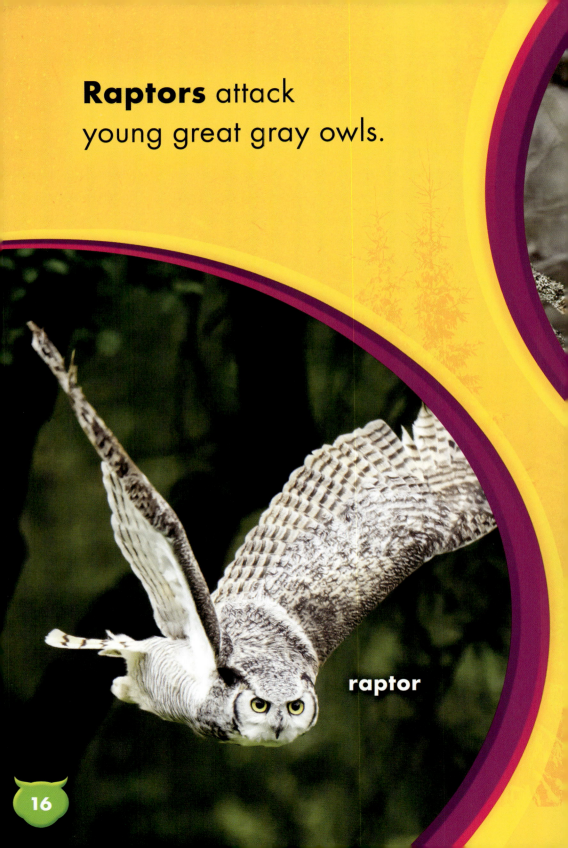

raptor

Adult owls keep their young safe. They hoot and snap their beaks at **predators**!

# Beyond Hunting

nest

In the spring, great gray owls find nests. They often use nests made by other birds.

Females lay up to five eggs at a time.

**Owlets** leave the nest early. They climb trees and practice flying.

In a few months, the **fledglings** are ready to hunt on their own!

owlet

# Growing Up

**1** egg — 28 to 36 days

**2** owlet — 3 to 4 weeks

**3** fledgling — around 6 weeks

life span: around 13 years

# Glossary

**fledglings**—young owls that have feathers for flight

**meadows**—fields of grass

**owlets**—baby owls

**perches**—places to sit or rest above the ground

**predators**—animals that hunt other animals for food

**prey**—animals that are hunted by other animals for food

**raptors**—large birds that hunt other animals; raptors have excellent eyesight and powerful talons.

**rodents**—small animals that gnaw on their food; mice, rats, and squirrels are all rodents.

**talons**—the strong, sharp claws of owls and other raptors

**wingspans**—measurements of the distance from the tip of one wing to the tip of the other wing

# To Learn More

## AT THE LIBRARY

Albertson, Al. *Great Gray Owls*. Minneapolis, Minn.: Bellwether Media, 2020.

Neunfeldt, Elizabeth. *Barn Owls*. Minneapolis, Minn.: Bellwether Media, 2024.

Whipple, Annette. *Whooo Knew? The Truth About Owls*. New York, N.Y.: Reycraft Books, 2020.

## ON THE WEB

### FACTSURFER

Factsurfer.com gives you a safe, fun way to find more information.

1. Go to www.factsurfer.com.

2. Enter "great gray owls" into the search box and click 🔍.

3. Select your book cover to see a list of related content.

# Index

adult, 17
attack, 16
beaks, 7, 9, 17
climb, 20
colors, 5, 7, 9
dive, 14
eggs, 19
eyes, 7, 9
faces, 6, 9
feathers, 5, 7, 9, 11
females, 19
fledglings, 20
fly, 11, 14, 20
food, 13, 14, 15
forests, 4
growing up, 21
hearing, 12, 13, 14
hoot, 17
hunt, 12, 14, 20
meadows, 14

nests, 18, 20
owlets, 20
perches, 14
predators, 17
prey, 14
range, 4, 5
raptors, 16
safe, 17
size, 8, 9, 10, 11
snow, 13
spring, 18
talons, 14
wingspan, 10, 11
young, 16, 17

The images in this book are reproduced through the courtesy of: Teresa Melcer, front cover; Eric Isselee, p. 3; MarclSchauer, p. 4; Miroslav Srb, p. 6; imageBROKER.com, p. 7; Giedriius, p. 8; Peter Krejzl, p. 9; Tomas Drahos, p. 10; Erik Mandre, pp. 11, 21 (top middle); Glass and Nature, p. 12; Nick Pecker, pp. 13 (top), 15 (top left); Erni, p. 13 (bottom); Ian Duffield, p. 14; Rolf Kopfle/ Alamy, pp. 14-15; photographybyJHWILLIAMS, p. 15 (top right); Ondrej Chavatal, p. 16; Wirestock, Inc./ Alamy, p. 17; Andrey V Vyalkov, p. 18; Krzysztof Baranowski/ Getty Images, p. 19; KAR Photography/ Alamy, p. 20; agefotostock/ Alamy, pp. 20-21; Michael Quinton/ Minden Pictures, p. 21 (top left); Ghost Bear, pp. 21 (top right), 22.